LDS GUITAR HYMNS
VOLUME ONE

Arranged by Dan Bunker

Cover Design by Spencer Jacobs

ISBN 978-0-9826198-2-7

ROYAL CIRQUE
PUBLISHING

www.royalcirquepub.com

PO Box 712151
Salt Lake City, UT 84171

Table of Contents

Guitar in Religious Settings

Many people consider the guitar an inappropriate instrument to be used in religious settings. While it is true that a Les Paul or a Stratocaster may not be the most reverent instrument, an acoustic guitar certainly can be. A nylon string classical guitar has a fine warm and mellow sound that allows this instrument to be as acceptable as a piano or violin in a religious setting.

Even though the classical guitar is acceptable in a sacred setting, check with your local church leaders before performing. Some individuals may feel guitar music to be inappropriate in a church meeting. This concern needs to be resolved with the proper authorities first rather than cause confrontation. The goal of any guitarist is to excite people about the guitar and its many uses.

The hymns in this book have been arranged for solo classical guitar. These pieces can be played in sacrament meetings, firesides, devotionals, or any other church related meeting needing or wanting instrumental music. Many of these hymns are in the same key so you can play a medley or you can repeat a certain hymn multiple times. See the appendix in this book for hymns that are grouped by music key, tunings, and time signatures.

A classical guitar is not the loudest instrument, especially when played in large rooms or halls. To have the guitar heard in these types of settings you have four practical choices.

1. You can use a classical guitar with a pickup in it to play through the room or hall's PA system. Many church chapels and other large rooms have a PA system. You simply need to get a cable that has a 1/4 inch plug on one side and a microphone XLR plug on the other. You can then control sound and volume from your pickup controls on the guitar.

2. You can mic the guitar by placing a microphone (attached to the room or hall's PA system) near the sound hole of the guitar.

3. You can use a classical guitar with a pickup in it (or mic it) and play through a guitar amplifier. This should be your last resort since guitar amplifiers are a visual icon of rock and roll and can detract from the sacred setting. Classical guitarists playing with the New York Philharmonic Orchestra don't have a Marshal Stack sitting behind them.

4. You can play loud enough or hope that the audience is quiet enough that the guitar can be heard on its own without requiring any kind of amplification.

How to Use This Book

Song Keys

The hymns chosen for this book have been transposed into music keys suitable for play on the guitar. As such, if you decide you want to accompany vocalists while playing these hymns, you may want to consider using a capo to adjust the key to match the vocalist's range.

Many of the hymns have been arranged in the same music key. You can create medleys of hymns easily by ending one hymn and then starting a new hymn in the same key. Be creative and add some bridging music to transition into the new hymn. You could also bridge or transition to a new hymn in another key if you want to get creative. See the Appendix for a listing of hymns grouped by key and time signature.

Guitar Tuning

The majority of the hymns in this book are in standard guitar tuning (E, A, D, G, B, E). There are a handful of arrangements in drop D tuning (D, A, D, G, B, E). This was done to ease the playing difficulty as well as improve the overall sound of the song. Each hymn lists the tuning in the upper left hand corner.

- For an explanation of Guitar Tunings visit http://en.wikipedia.org/wiki/Guitar_tuning

Notation

Each piece is notated in staff, tablature, and chord diagrams. Use whatever notation system is easiest for you to follow. The chord diagrams are rough guides to help you see fingering positions. These diagrams should be used as guides only since the melody often moves outside of the basic chord structure.

- For an explanation of Staff Notation visit http://en.wikipedia.org/wiki/Musical_notation
- For an explanation of Tablature Notation visit http://en.wikipedia.org/wiki/Tablature
- For an explanation of Chord Diagrams visit http://en.wikipedia.org/wiki/Guitar_chord

Picking

These hymns should be played with your fingers and not a pick. All of the arrangements have been created in the classical guitar style.

Other Resources

If you would like to hear each of these hymns, mp3's can be purchased at a discounted price from http://www.ldsguitarhymns.com. As the owner of this book, type in the code A2X-D4EE to receive a 50% discount on the recorded music pieces that are in this book. If you are struggling with some of the rhythms, listening to the pieces is a good way to help perfect your playing.

- You can also contact the author at http://www.ldsguitarhymns.com.

Abide With Me!

Standard Tuning
E, A, D, G, B, E

Willian H. Monk
Arranged by Dan Bunker

A Poor Wayfaring Man Of Grief

George Coles
Arranged by Dan Bunker

Standard Tuning
E, A, D, G, B, E

Come, Come, Ye Saints

Willian Clayton
Arranged by Dan Bunker

Drop D Tuning
D, A, D, G, B, E

Come, Follow Me

Samuel McBurney
Arranged by Dan Bunker

Did You Think To Pray?

Standard Tuning
E, A, D, G, B, E

Willian O. Perkins
Arranged by Dan Bunker

For The Beauty Of The Earth

Conrad Kocher
Arranged by Dan Bunker

Standard Tuning
E, A, D, G, B, E

♩ = 120 Joyfully

God Be With You Till We Meet Again

Willian G. Tomer
Arranged by Dan Bunker

Standard Tuning
E, A, D, G, B, E

How Firm A Foundation

Standard Tuning
E, A, D, G, B, E

J. Ellis
Arranged by Dan Bunker

How Firm A Foundation

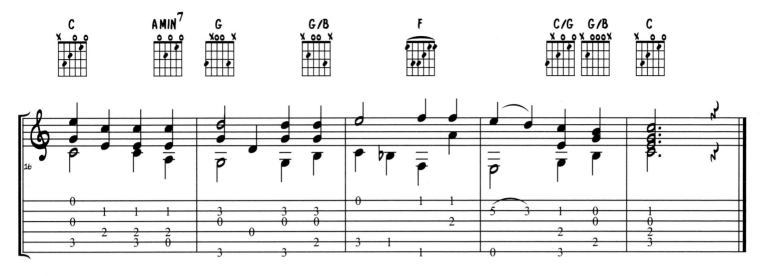

High On The Mountain Top

Standard Tuning
E, A, D, G, B, E

Ebeneezer Beesley
Arranged by Dan Bunker

I Know That My Redeemer Lives

Standard Tuning
E, A, D, G, B, E

Lewis D. Edwards
Arranged by Dan Bunker

I Need Thee Every Hour

Drop D Tuning
D, A, D, G, B, E

Robert Lowry
Arranged by Dan Bunker

Israel, Israel, God Is Calling

Drop D Tuning
D, A, D, G, B, E

Charles C. Converse
Arranged by Dan Bunker

JOSEPH SMITH'S FIRST PRAYER

Sylvanus Billings Pond
Arranged by Dan Bunker

Standard Tuning
E, A, D, G, B, E

More Holiness Give Me

Nearer, My God, To Thee

Drop D Tuning
D, A, D, G, B, E

Lowell Mason
Arranged by Dan Bunker

O My Father

Standard Tuning
E, A, D, G, B, E

James McGranahan
Arranged by Dan Bunker

Praise To The Man

Standard Tuning
E, A, D, G, B, E

Scottish Folk Song
Arranged by Dan Bunker

Praise To The Man

24

Redeemer Of Israel

Freeman Lewis
Arranged by Dan Bunker

Drop D Tuning
D, A, D, G, B, E

There Is A Green Hill Far Away

John H. Gower
Arranged by Dan Bunker

Standard Tuning
E, A, D, G, B, E

We Are Sowing

Standard Tuning
E, A, D, G, B, E

Henry A. Tuckett
Arranged by Dan Bunker

Common Chords Used In This Book

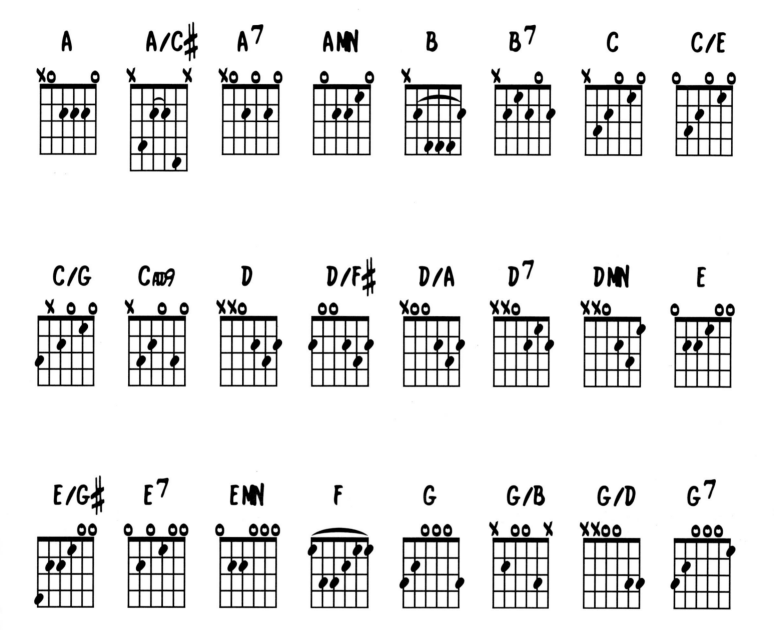

Appendix
Hymns by Key and Time Signature

Key of A	Time Signature
Abide With Me!	4/4
Did You Think To Pray?	4/4
High On The Mountain Top	2/2
More Holiness Give Me	4/4
O My Father	3/4

Key of C	Time Signature
A Poor Wayfaring Man Of Grief	6/8
For The Beauty Of The Earth	4/4
How Firm A Foundation	4/4
We Are Sowing	3/4

Key of D	Time Signature
Come, Come, Ye Saints	4/4
I Know That My Redeemer Lives	4/4
I Need Thee Every Hour	3/4
Nearer, My God, To Thee	4/4

Key of E	Time Signature
Joseph Smith's First Prayer	4/4

Key of G	Time Signature
Come, Follow Me	3/4
God Be With You Till We Meet Again	4/4
Israel, Israel, God Is Calling	4/4
Praise To The Man	2/4
Redeemer Of Israel	4/4
There Is A Green Hill Far Away	4/4

Performance Notes

Performance Notes

ROYAL CIRQUE
PUBLISHING

www.royalcirquepub.com

CLASSICAL GUITAR ARRANGEMENTS
for 20 Favorite LDS Hymns.

These Hymns have been selected from the Church of Jesus Christ of Latter Day Saint Hymn Book. Regardless of your playing ability you will be able to find a piece in this book that is appropriate to play at any setting. Whether in Church or at home you will bring the familiar sounds of LDS Hymns to others through the warm sounds of the guitar.

❧ Hymns are listed by Music Key so they can be grouped together and played in a medley.

❧ All scores contain Tab, Staff, and Chord Diagrams to aid all types and levels of players.

❧ Improve you classical guitar playing skills and fingerpicking skills.

ROYAL CIRQUE
PUBLISHING

www.royalcirquepub.com

PO Box 712151
Salt Lake City, UT 84171

$17.95
ISBN 978-0-9826198-2-7
51795>

9 780982 619827